I0213673

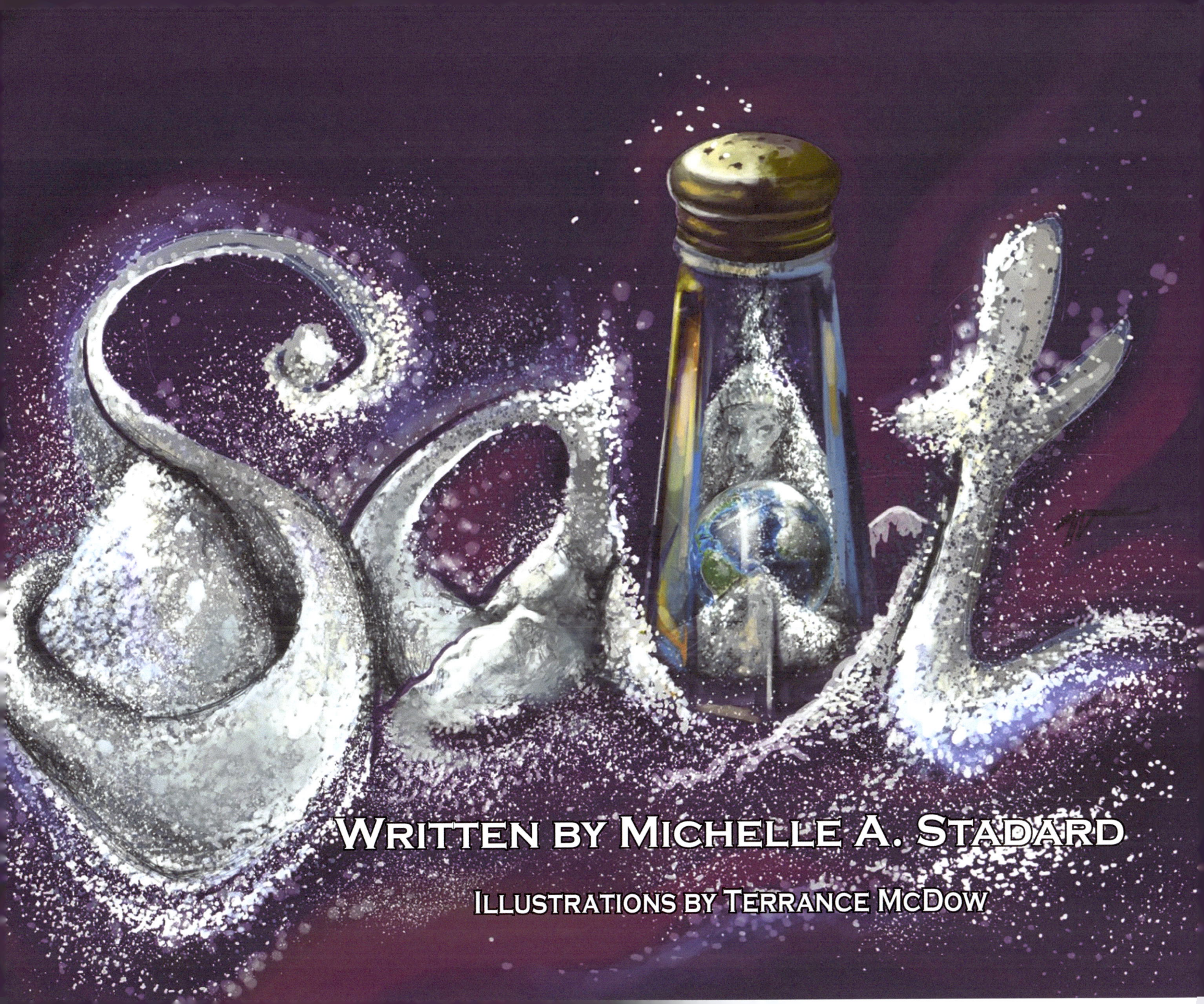

Salt

WRITTEN BY MICHELLE A. STADARD

ILLUSTRATIONS BY TERRANCE MCDOW

SALT

Copyright © 2023—Michelle A. Stadard

ALL RIGHTS RESERVED UNDER U.S., LATIN AMERICAN AND INTERNATIONAL COPYRIGHT CONVENTIONS

Unless otherwise noted, all Scripture references are from the *Holy Bible, King James Version,* public domain. References marked "NIV" are from the *Holy Bible, New International Version,* copyright © 1973, 1978, 1984 by International Bible Society, Colorado Springs, Colorado.

Illustrations by Terrance McDow

Published by:

McDougal & Associates

18896 Greenwell Springs Road

Greenwell Springs, LA 70739

www.ThePublishedWord.com

McDougal & Associates is an organization dedicated to spreading the Gospel of the Lord Jesus Christ to as many people as possible in the shortest time possible.

ISBN: 978-1-950398-86-7

Printed On Demand

For Worldwide Distribution

Dedication

This book is dedicated:

To all servants of God: Keep working because only what you do for Him will last.

To my family and friends: Thanks for supporting me in all I do. You know who you are. Continue loving one another and being the Salt of the Earth.

In loving Memory of Leslie Renee Hodge for her words of encouragement and for pushing me to finish the work. You are forever in my heart.

Acknowledgments

First and foremost, I want to acknowledge God for giving me the gift of penmanship and for chastising me to love correctly and be the salt. I thank Him for loving me enough to allow me to pour into His people.

A special thank you to my husband, Odimir, for putting up with me and encouraging me not to give up, but to always pursue my dreams. I love you, Babe!

Contents

1. Start Applying Love Today 7

2. Applying Pressure 15

3. Learning Obedience 19

4. Persevering in Pushing 25

5. Letting Love Cover 29

6. Getting Started...37

7. Applying Yourself..41

8. Loving Enough 45

9. Realizing that Today Is the Day...51

Author Contact Information... 52

Other Books by Michelle A. Stadard.......................................53

Chapter 1

Start Applying Love Today--SALT

Salt has an extraordinarily rich background, has been used as far back as our ancient world, and still carries its strength and importance today. Salt was an important gem in the ancient world because of its many uses. There was a point when people were actually using salt as money for trading. It was also widely used because it helped to preserve food, especially meats, which were often the first foods to spoil. Salt also helps wounds to heal faster.

The scientific name for salt is sodium, and it appears in the Periodic Table of elements as such (Na). Salt is one of the greatest elements in the world and one of the main ingredients in our foods. Therefore, it is quite necessary for cooking.

Cooking requires food seasonings, and without salt being one of those seasonings, a dish would be incomplete and unsavory. Salt is a flavor enhancer and, in general, puts the final touch on foods. As a cook, I begin to add all my seasonings—such as pepper, basil, and thyme—to the pot. But adding all those seasonings does not amount to a hill of beans if I don't remember to put the salt in the pot along with them. If the salt is forgotten, the food will be plain or bland, and the result will be unhappy and disgruntled customers. Salt flavors the food and gives it life. It wakes up all the other flavors, and before you know it, you have a tasty dish.

Salt can also be a cook's downfall. Using not enough salt can bring a dish to ruin, but the same applies to the over-usage of salt. Too much salt can cause you to have to throw out expensive foods and suffer the loss of the monies invested. You need just the right amount of salt added to a dish to prevent waste. Using a measuring spoon or tool when cooking can be helpful with this. Salt gives the food the love that makes customers say, "Mmmm, good" every time and keeps them coming back for more.

I am speaking from experience. Many years ago, I once had so much on my mind that I forgot to add salt to my pot of food, and it turned out bland. Many leftovers ended up in the trash. The mother of one of my friends commented, "Michelle, what happened? I know your food can taste better than that."

I said "Yeah, I know. I forgot to add the salt to my pot." This reminds me of the passage of scripture found in the Word of God where it talks about salt:

If the salt has lost it savor [flavor abilities to make it tasty, saltiness], how can it be salted again? It is worthless but to be trodden [useless] under the feet of men.

Matthew 5:13

We, as ambassadors of Christ, must do all we can to be the salt of the earth.

Have you figured out yet what salt is? Salt is God's love, and He wants us to love His way and on His terms.

You might ask, "What does it mean to do things God's way?" It is letting go of your own ways and your own ways of thinking and choosing God's ways instead. Only the way He thinks matters.

At one point, some years ago, there was a slogan going around: "What Would Jesus Do?" or WWJD? This is an important question for every man and woman who names the name of Jesus.

When following Christ, the Son of the living God, salt is, again, a necessary nutrient to qualify us as a representative (follower). It is mentioned repeatedly throughout the Bible. One of the more well-known passages on salt is found in what are called The Beatitudes. I like to call them The Beautiful Attitudes:

You are the salt [my representatives] of the earth. But if the salt loses its saltiness, how can it be salty again? It is no longer good for anything, except thrown out and trampled underfoot. **Matthew 5:13**

Believers in Christ must be examples and live by showing others God's ways. We are, indeed, the salt of the earth.

What does it mean to be the salt of the earth? It means to be like Christ. It means not to be a part of the world, conforming to it and its standards, but to be a preservative, an example to others.

And what does that involve? It involves staying rooted and grounded in the Word of God and showing love to others by doing God's will.

As noted, salt is known best as a food enhancer. It adds more flavor and really wakes up your food dishes. As followers (disciples) of Christ and believers of God, we must maintain our flavor, being the salters of the earth, allowing God (the Source of all things) to keep supplying us with the salt necessary to influence His Kingdom and align with His will.

Many times we allow things to get in our paths, and they cause us stagnation. In my case, it was the fact that my sister and I were at odds with one another for years. We could not seem to get along. When we were with other people, we put up a good front, but behind closed doors, it was a broken relationship.

It was, as we say, "tore up from the floor up, looking at it from the outside in." Things may have appeared all good, but that was not the case at all, not by a long shot. It was not until my vow renewal that things were made right.

I thank God that when we allow Him to fix things, He does it right (righteously).

As believers, we must also be careful of the voices that we allow to feed our spirits. I experienced a negative voice trying to feed my spirit, telling me that reconciliation with my sister would never happen, basically, that my relationship with my sister was doomed. I can say that the enemy was and still is a liar. I gave God His words back and prayed, believed, and trusted Him to perform the work, and He did.

At first, it seemed like it would never happen, the fights grew worse, and every encounter was terrible. But we know Satan's tactics, and one of them is illusion.

Another is fear:

> <u>F</u>alse
> <u>E</u>lements
> <u>A</u>ppearing
> <u>R</u>eal

The enemy uses fear to steal a believer's joy. God must remain at the center of our world.

When we keep our focus on Him, we can see His hand working things out for us, and nothing else matters.

My sister consented to be my matron of honor, and we were reconciled. I give God glory and honor because He worked it all out. Move yourself out of the situation, take your hands off of it, and allow God to work it out.

God tells us in His Word:

All things are possible to him that believes.

Mark 9:23

This was one of my favorite passages as a child, and I still hold it dear today and try to live by it.

Salt should be applied in our daily relationships with our neighbors. Neighbors are not just people who live next door to us; they are anyone and everyone we meet.

We are made in God's similitude, in His likeness, which is from the best "stuff" ever known. That reminds me of the Snapple's slogan "Made from the best stuff on earth." In our case, it is not from the earth. We are made from heavenly material and, therefore, we are divine.

We must get busy enhancing everyone we meet with this good "stuff." We must live by God's message and tell others about Him, showing them how by our attitude and the way we treat one another.

Love has always been an action word. It has never been just a word. Love is based on what is done. An individual can tell you all day, "I love you," and it still does not mean anything if that love is never shown.

The question is asked, "How much do You love me? "This much," He answers. Then He stretched out His arms and died for you and me. We can see Jesus' picture displayed on the cross all over the world. The account of the cross … we all know it and are remarkably familiar with it. God's reconciliation, His ultimate plan to win His people back unto Himself was realized through Jesus' sacrifice. God's love, as it was and is shown to us, is priceless and cannot be bought, and He showed us His love by sending His only Son to be the ultimate sacrifice.

Salt is seen throughout the Word of God in the fact that many of God's people allowed Him to be the Source from which their salt came. God is still the Source, or what today we call our Supplier.

There is so much energy in God. When I start thinking of an outlet and things being plugged into that outlet, power is being transferred from that outlet through that plug and into the individual devices. God is our Source, and power is transferred from Him to us and through us to others. Without the Source, everything would be dead.

God's love is the salt we need. It all derives from His Spirit, which should dwell in the hearts of His people. The Supplier and Source of this salt is only waiting for our submission, which is a yes on our part. Our yes signifies obedience to the will of God. God doesn't need anything from us. He is the Creator of all and is in all. He waits for a yes, which is from the free will He gave to His human creatures. Humans are the only creatures that were made with it.

It was said repeatedly, "If we tell God our plans, He begins to laugh." Remember: Sarah and Abraham had their plans. They were thinking in their heads that somehow they would help God with His promise. For some reason, He was taking too long. But God does everything in decency and in order. He knows all, and very often we make a bigger mess of things when we fail to wait on His timing. Many times our impatience causes us a lot of trouble. God's timing is the very best timing. He is time, in time, on time, through time, and was the Preeminent before time.

Adultery is a sin, so God knew that would not be the route to provide Abraham a son. He had another way that was sweet, and that way was to open Sarah's barren womb.

Of course, Sarah despised Hagar and didn't want her around anymore. Why? Because she had "messed with" her husband. But that was Sarah's own fault for being impatient and suggesting this liaison.

We, God's people, can be messy at times, but God knows our thoughts, and He knows when to step in and fix things. He doesn't need us to help Him do anything. Everything is based and runs off the will that God has for our lives. Don't be tricked into thinking and don't let anyone tell you it doesn't. Get with the plan and prosper.

You are the salt
[my representatives]
of the earth.
But if the salt loses its saltiness,
how can it be salty again?
It is no longer good for anything,
except thrown out
and trampled underfoot.

—Matthew 5:13

Chapter 2

Applying Pressure

When it comes to a wound, the first advice someone in the medical profession will give is this: "Apply pressure to that wound." Applying pressure will isolate the injury. If the wound is bleeding, the pressure may well stop the flow of blood to that area. Pressure should be kept against the wound until the individual can get proper medical attention.

If pressure is not applied to the area of a wound, the individual could face even bigger problems. The wound could get messier, and there is always the risk of the individual losing too much blood. It could end up soaking through their clothing or using many more gauzes or bandages than expected.

The same applies with our walk with God. Pressure is vitally necessary in our daily relationship with Him. Pressure will guarantee a rightful relationship with God. We can apply this pressure by studying His Word.

Prayer is another key for communication, to stay in fellowship and rightful position with our Creator. Fasting is another discipline that helps us to keep the pressure on. There are many more spiritual disciplines that can help us keep pressure applied.

The apostle Paul wrote:

The weapons we fight with are not the weapons of the world. On the contrary, they have divine power to demolish strongholds, we demolish arguments and every pretension that sets itself up against the knowledge of God, and we take captive every thought to make it obedient to Christ.

2 Corinthians 10:4-5

When I was in the U.S. Army and was in training, we used some of the most powerful weapons in the world. We would go into a room filled with what the Army calls "weaponeers." These are dummy weapons we could use to practice our individual shooting skills. The purpose was to train soldiers until it was time for them to go to the shooting range to qualify with real weapons.

The enemy is on the prowl, still looking to devour the chosen of God. We must never become complacent or get caught in his traps. Pressure can burst pipes, and our spiritual pressure can defeat Satan, our enemy.

What can we do? We are to *"put on the whole armor of God"*:

Put on the whole armor of God, that ye may be able to stand against the wiles of the devil.

Ephesians 6:11

We have spiritual weapons to use against the enemy. This fight is spiritual and has been raging since the beginning of time. Obedience is needed and is one of the weapons that are mighty and vital to our spiritual warfare. The Word of God tells us:

Submit to God and resist the devil and he will flee.

James 4:7

If we can get out of self, that is the first step in being obedient. Christ is the perfect example of this. The Word also tells us what we must do first:

Then Jesus said to His disciples, "If anyone wants to come after Me, let him deny himself, and take up his cross, and be following Me."

Matthew 16:24-25

Jesus denied Himself and was beaten, ridiculed, and eventually crucified:

Being found in appearance as a man, He humbled Himself by becoming obedient to the point of death, even death on a cross.

Philippians 2:8

Your obedience to the will of God will cost you, but the reward will always be greater than your sufferings.

THE WEAPONS WE FIGHT WITH ARE NOT THE WEAPONS OF THE WORLD. ON THE CONTRARY, THEY HAVE DIVINE POWER TO DEMOLISH STRONGHOLDS.
— 2 Corinthians 10:4-5

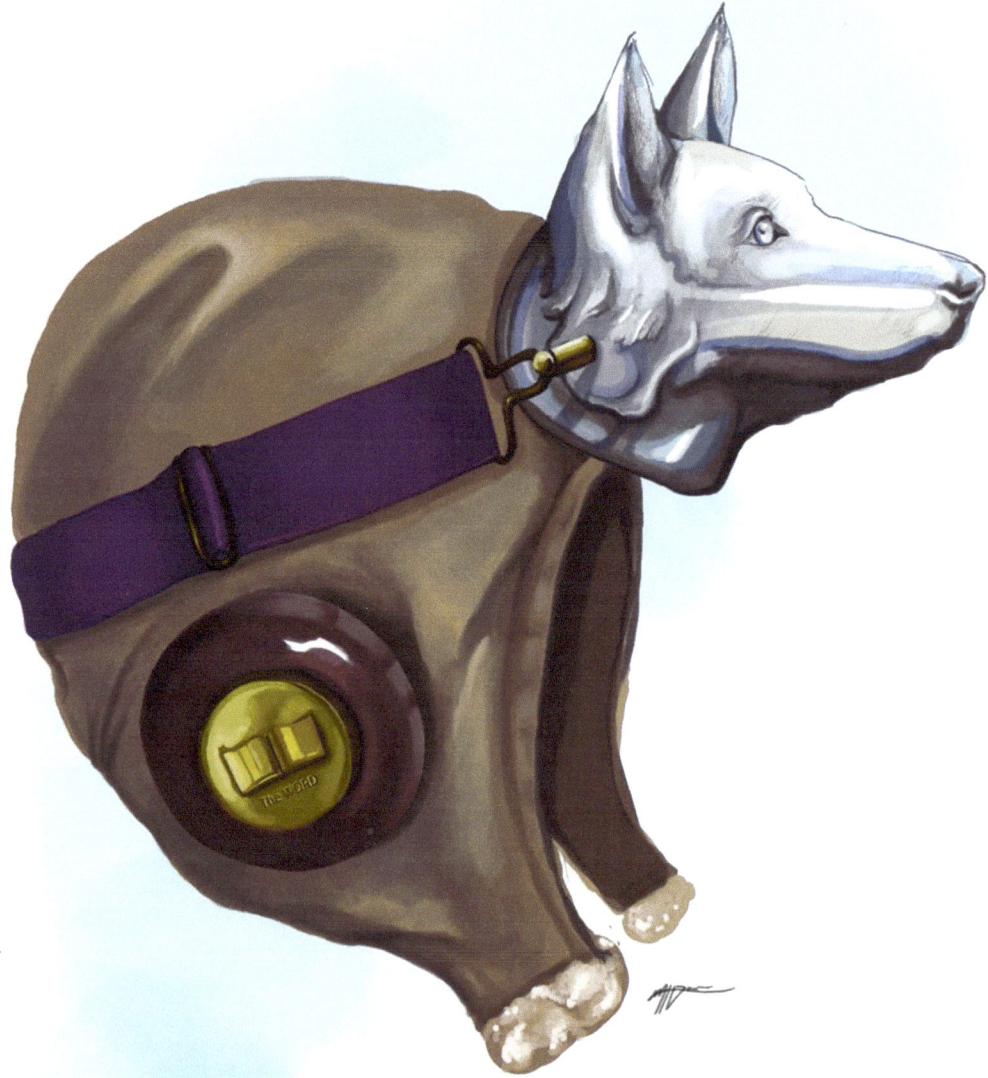

Learning Obedience

Obedience can be defined as "compliance with an order, request, or law, or submission to another's authority." In the Christian life, obedience is a requirement and is important to our being "the salt of the earth." There is an old wise saying: "You can lead a horse to the water, but you cannot make him drink." In other words, you can give someone wise counsel, but it is up to that individual whether he or she follows the advice given. In the words of a psalter in the Scriptures:

Do not be like the horse or the mule, which have no understanding but must be controlled by bit and bridle or they will not come to you. **Psalm 32:9**

We must obey God willingly and consistently. He made us a little different than the rest of His creations. He created us with the ability to exercise free will. This means that things are never forced; God gives us a choice to serve Him or Satan. Obedience is better than sacrifice, as we know, have heard, and can attest to:

So, Samuel said: "Has the LORD as great delight in burnt offerings and sacrifices, as in obeying the voice of the LORD? Behold, to obey is better than sacrifice, and to heed than the fat of rams." **1 Samuel 15:22**

Salt must obey in order to be used by the Salter (God), and obedience is the key.

When I was in the military, I often heard my drill sergeants yelling, telling us soldiers to stay alert. If the soldiers remained alert, could listen clearly and see the enemy or other dangers approaching.

Watching your surroundings was also vital. This meant staying on guard. As with the natural, so with the spiritual. We are to be on guard in the Spirit always:

Be sober, be vigilant; because your adversary the devil, as a roaring lion, walketh about, seeking whom he may devour.   1 Peter 5:8

The drill sergeant would then add the phrase, "Stay Alive!" The purpose was to discuss the dangers that could be met in training or in times of war. There was always the possibility of the enemy taking over the entire camp and capturing us as prisoners of war (POWs). Staying alive was of extreme importance, so we had to listen to the things that would help us to survive and make it back home in one piece.

Soldiers must be willing to obey. This means listening to and adhering to orders and commands given by instructors. In our case, the instructors were the drill sergeants. They were the authority figures who watched over us. Each soldier had to go through Basic Training, which included intense and difficult training that usually lasted nine weeks or more.

During Basic Training, soldiers receive necessary skills for surviving combat (war). If a soldiers yields, listening to and obeying the instructions given by those drill sergeants, when the training is completed, those soldiers can graduate and move on to the next level of training. This is called AIT or IT, in my case—Army Individual Training.

Many accidents occur in the military because of friendly fire. I was nearly a victim of such an accident, but God spared me. I have had my own experiences, so when I stress to you how important it is to obey and follow instructions, I know what I'm talking about. This is also necessary to remain the salt of the earth.

There is a story I often tell when I feel like it needs to be heard. This will be my first time to put it on paper.

While in Basic Training, we were at the rifle range for marksmanship qualifications, in layman's terms, "to see how well we could shoot a weapon." The drill sergeants constantly stressed to all of us soldiers, while down on the range, getting weapons checked to make sure there was no brass or ammo left in them. The purpose was to ensure safety and make sure all weapons were clear, leaving nothing stuck in them when it came time to shoot them in the "shakedown phase."

This inspection would also ensure that soldiers were not carrying any ammo back to the barracks or any other place besides where it needed to go, and that was the designated areas, the amnesty boxes. Many times, brass and live ammo can get stuck in a soldier's weapon. If not detected quickly, this can cause injuries.

On this particular day, while we were down at the rifle range training, there was one soldier who didn't want to listen to the drill sergeant's instructions. She decided she was not going to obey. She skipped all the amnesty check lines, which were down range. She passed by every drill instructor that was ensuring weapons safety with a no-brass-and-no-ammo policy. She made it to the last station, which was the clearing-of-your-weapons line. In that line, soldiers would actually fire their weapon to ensure there was nothing in it.

I was in the front line of soldiers, and this soldier was directly behind me. The command was given to put the weapons on "Blast." The next thing I recalled was the drill sergeants running and yelling and pulling me off the range, asking me over and over if I was okay, and expressing how sorry they were.

I immediately knew that God had sent His angels to cover me.

The bullet, which had fired from that soldier's gun was an M16 A2. It flew dangerously close to my head, but it had not harmed me at all. I heard it scream past me. That bullet could very easily have blown my head to smithereens. It was a "but God" moment. My life was spared, and I was grateful.

Many people can say they have experienced miracles. This was mine. God showed me how He, Elohim Shomri, was my Protector.

As you can imagine, the soldier who accidentally fired that shot got chewed out and reprimanded for disobedience and negligence that could have cost me my life. Obedience is a requirement that must be honored, for it can create a life-or-death situation. You must, as stressed earlier, be willing to obey in order to properly be used by the Salter. God wants to hear us say the words, "Yes, Lord, I want to be used in the earth for Your glory."

One of my favorite songs was written by the Gospel group Shekinah Glory. It is about a believer "messing up" by doing things her own way on her own terms. It wasn't until she repented and surrendered to God and His will that things began to align right in her life. One of the verses says "If You lead me, I'll go," and "yes" is repeated over and over in the song. It is clearly a message about obedience to the Lord.

Obedience is not always easy, for it involves giving up something. For believers, there must be a continuance of obedience as it relates to God's will. This requires the individual to be able to use wisdom. There are two types of wisdom—godly and worldly. The guidance of God's Spirit will lead you in the ways of truth. Godly wisdom will enable you to make right choices. Many times, this is not easy, and we need to be able to fight temptations. You can fight them successfully only through the Word of God.

When Jesus came off of His many days of fasting and consecration before His Father, the enemy was there to tempt Him:

Now when the tempter came to Him, he said, "If You are the Son of God, command that these stones become bread."

But He answered and said, "It is written, 'Man shall not live by bread alone, but by every word that proceeds from the mouth of God.'" Matthew 4:3-4

At once and without hesitation, Jesus used the Word of God as His defense. The same applies to us. The Salter waits on us to give up our selfishness and totally give in to Him.

MAN SHALL NOT LIVE BY BREAD ALONE, BUT BY EVERY WORD THAT PROCEEDS FROM THE MOUTH OF GOD.
— Matthew 4:4

Chapter 4

Persevering in Pushing

Pushing is of extreme importance and is a requirement to become the salt of the earth.

I was part of my high school track team, and while on the team, I took part in several major events. I remember most running the four-by-four relay race. In the four-by-four, there was a lot of running involved. Each individual had to be able to endure until the race was over. That was the whole purpose. We had to push past things that might seem to slow us up or even stop us or prevent us from finishing the race.

There were many things a runner could experience to disqualify, distract, or keep them from finishing. Their body got extremely tired and even cramped up, and this could slow them down, discourage them, or even prevent them from finishing.

One year, while I was watching the Olympics on TV, they did a flashback segment on Derek Redmond, an Olympian from years before. He was remembered for his endurance and courage. They showed a clip from his race, and toward the end of it, he tore a hamstring.

Derek was devastated. This injury would prevent him from wining. However, he mustered up the strength to push past everything his body was experiencing and continue toward the finish line. As he neared the end, his father ran out onto the track and helped him across the finish line.

One day, when I was running, my high school track coach yelled, "Come on, Williams, push!" At the time, I was extremely exhausted and nearly ready to quit. He encouraged me by cheering me on and helped me hang in there. I pushed a little more, gave it all I had, and was able to finish.

This same determination is needed to be the salt that God (the Salter) wants us to be in the earth. Many times, it may seem difficult to push. We must push past the pain because we know that there is "purpose in our pain," my sister and fellow author, Angie Taylor Reames, has told us.

One of the common commands given by doctors in labor and delivery rooms is for you to push. I had two natural births, and the rest of them were by cesarean section (better known as a C-section or C-cuts). In childbirth, a lot of pushing is necessary, but after pushing past all the pain, a beautiful bundle of joy is birthed. Your baby is delivered.

After the delivery, you realize that the pain you were experiencing was only temporary and was necessary. The same is true for those who wish to excel and move on to the next levels in Christ. Pushing through the distress and finishing the race should be the top priority in our walk with God. Pushing helps us develop endurance within, ad that makes all the difference.

Do not be like the horse
or the mule,
which have no understanding
but must be controlled
by bit and bridle
or they will not
come to you.

—Psalm 32:9

Chapter 5

Letting Love Cover

Love covers because it protects you from danger and anything that might harm or damage you. Love covers because it overlooks, and it endures. Salt faithfully continues to do what it is purposed to do. Love conquers because it moves mountains, things that seem impossible, things that cannot happen unless they are done by a miracle of the hand of God. But these things are only impossible in the eyes of man. With God, all things are possible to him who believes (see Mark 9:23). Jesus said to His disciples:

For verily I say unto you, That whosoever shall say unto this mountain, Be thou removed, and be thou cast into the sea; and shall not doubt in his heart, but shall believe that those things which he saith shall come to pass; he shall have whatsoever he saith. Mark 11:23

Many times we face mountains in our lives It could be family issues that seem just as big as any mountains we might see, family issues that continue to the next generations.

Many times, we give the enemy way too much power over our lives. Too often we let him come in. It could be through a small misunderstanding that might have been settled through a simple conversation. Such a discussion can settle a miscommunication and stop the bleeding and resulting curses in the bloodlines. Sadly, separations come, and you have little groups within the family. Clearly, this should not be happening. We must be willing to be the salt of the earth and let it permeate everything in our lives. Love is what is done by our actions, not what is said by our mouths.

Family misunderstandings, if not dealt with, become mountains, obstacles that are in the way to stop the move of God in your family. The enemy knows this and sees the potential to harm the family. There is strength in unity. United we stand, but divided we fall.

Deception tricks the mind, and many times a person is not dealing with an actual family member, but with something that happened weeks, months, or even years before, even before that individual's time. This is deception out of control. Sadly, many times we allow such things to go unresolved for years and years, instead of facing those mountains. The result is that the conflict passes on to the next generations, and the bloodline is cursed because the members can't work together as God intended.

Such mountains can be removed through prayer. We know that mountains are not easily moved. In fact, in the natural, they are impossible to move by own efforts. But we know that with God's Spirit living in us and working through us, it can happen.

God has given us the power to declare and speak a thing into existence, and He can move all the mountains in our lives ... if we will just allow Him to do it. He is omnipotent and spoke everything into existence that was ever made.

In the other half of that scripture, the part we seem to forget so easily, Jesus explained to His disciples *"and shall not doubt."* The Word of God tells us that it is impossible to please God without faith, because those who believe God must believe that He exists and is a rewarder of those who diligently seek Him (see Hebrews 11:6). Doubt cannot be a part of us.

Doubt tries to settle in, and at times our beliefs become shaky. Some actually stop believing the wonderful things our God can do.

He told the disciples that if they believed in their hearts, they would see mountains moved.

When we believe in our hearts that mountains (obstacles) can be removed and cast into the sea, God does the work. When we believe God, everything else becomes irrelevant. If something is not helping the situation, speak life into it. Words that are spoken negatively are hindrances and are of the enemy. Trust the Lord to see you through issues within your family, so that you are united and not divided.

When something takes place that is beyond our control, return it to the sender. Speak to that mountain, having the faith that you will move it and cast it into the sea. If we allow doubt to settle in, it will prevent the move of God. It is still His will that we be the salt of the earth.

Love must shine through our lives and spill over into the lives of others. How do you see the Gospel of Christ? In Hebrews, He tells us some Good News:

For indeed the gospel was preached to us as well as to them; but the word which they heard did not profit them, not being mixed with faith in those who heard it.

Hebrews 4:2

This Gospel is, without a doubt, Good News, the good news of God's love for His people. It tells us what God did to win the world back. It was His love that covered us. He loved us so much that He seasoned us with salt and then made us the salt of the earth.

His salt, His love, was applied and in action, and that is how we are to be the salt of the earth. We are to apply what He has given us to others by showing them that He lives in us. Doing this at every opportunity is vital.

Whatever the issues are, we can overcome through God's love. For example, if it is unforgiveness, we should pray always as the Word of God instructs us to do without ceasing (see 1 Thessalonians 5:17), praying that God will deal with our hearts and remove the root of whatever is causing the divisions.

Remembering what the Word of God has told us, that we are the salt of the earth, we must not allow the enemy to come in and take over our spirits.

Your example may be different. I used unforgiveness as a key issue among families. Often this is the root of family issues.

Peter, one of the disciples, asked Jesus a serious question:

Then Peter came to Jesus and asked, "Lord, how many times shall I forgive my brother who sins against me? Up to seven times?"

Matthew 18:21

This was not about a math problem. It was about an important principle. Jesus' answer is surprising:

Jesus said to him, "I do not say to you, up to seven times, but up to seventy times seven."

Matthew 18:22

"Seventy times seven?" That's 490 times. In other words, we are to forgive always, as long as you have God-given breath. When He gives us an opportunity to get things right, we should always forgive others and let them off the hook, just as God has forgiven us. Give to others the same grace that God has given to us.

This applies to all of us, and we should carefully obey it with all our hearts. There are issues that we walk around with in our hearts for years, and many times the other person knows nothing about how they may have harmed us. We must take everything to God. Why? Because He has the power to change things. If we try to manage things in our own strength, we are destined to fail. Turning things over to God, who can do all things but fail, is the best solution to all our problems.

Think about the big, beautiful glaciers and immovable rocky mountains we sometimes see from afar as we travel. Their appearance leaves us in awe every single time. We can, without a doubt, see the work of God in their creation, and we began to reflect on His awesomeness at creating such wonders in the earth. Those mountains don't move. But the mountains I'm speaking of in our lives are indeed movable … if we will just allow God to have His way in our hearts.

There is nothing too hard for God to do. We must apply the salt by speaking the Word of God: *"Mountain, be thou removed and be cast into the sea."* Words are powerful, and your words are even more powerful.

Remember the old cliche, "Sticks and stones may break my bones, but words will never hurt me." I'm here to tell you that this is an untruth from the very pits of Hell. Words do hurt and can do a lot of damage.

The Word of God tells us:

Life and death is in the power of the tongue.
Proverbs 18:21

What you speak out of your mouth will manifest. It could be positive and bring life and healing to a situation, or it can be negative, tearing down and destroying, bringing harm and death to a situation.

If we consider ourselves to be representatives of Christ, the salt of the earth, we should be speaking life into the atmosphere. Words that are spoken can stay with you for many years. Some words you never forget. They change you, for good or for bad.

My husband shared with me some negative words that were spoken to him in childhood. A certain individual told him he would "never be nothing," "never amount to much of anything." Those words were negative and could have crippled him for the rest of his life. Fortunately, he didn't let it happen. He went on to finish grade school and high school and then proudly served in the U.S. military. He went on to obtain his bachelor's degree, and is currently a supervisor in the career of his choice. If we refuse to allow negative words, which are weapons formed against us, to prosper, we will win every time. The enemy is put to shame when we use the Word of God to defeat him.

We must be mindful of what is coming out of our mouths. Words of wisdom build and never destroy. There was an old song we would often sing in the Pentecostal Church growing up. "Love Lifted Me." The chorus ended with the words, "When nothing else could help, love lifted me." That song says so much and should hit us every time we hear it.

God, the Source and Salter, sent Christ, His only Son, to be the salt of the earth. In this way, He showed His love, not through words, but pouring it out for all humanity through His actions. His ultimate sacrifice was enough to lift the sin debt and reconcile our broken relationship with the Father. Love conquers hate every time.

For verily I say unto you, That whosoever shall say unto this mountain, Be thou removed, and be thou cast into the sea; and shall not doubt in his heart, but shall believe that those things which he saith shall come to pass; he shall have whatsoever he saith.

— Mark 11:23

Chapter 6

Getting Started

There is old proverb: "The journey of a thousand miles begins with a single step." How will we know the outcome if we never start? We need to start by making up our minds to begin. Everything has a starting point. Before any great race or event, you can see the contestants lined up, and the judges or referees are saying, "On your mark." The next command is "Get set," and the last command is "Go!" What are you doing to change things in your situation? There are necessary steps to help you get there.

Admitting that there is a problem is one of the first steps to recovery. Are we taking our problems to God? Do we have a rightful relationship with Him? We can make a bigger mess of things by trying to carry the load alone, overseeing things alone. The answer is the Holy Spirit that God gives us freely. He can teach us how to start applying love today.

Being the salt requires not answering back when we find ourselves in the heat of a moment. The Word of God tells us:

A soft answer turns away wrath, but harsh words stir up anger.   Proverbs 15:1

One of the sayings in the military was "You are held accountable for your actions." God is only concerned about how we respond to life's situations. Not everything needs a response. Some may think you're weak for not answering back, but God knows you're strong.

When we are angry, we say a lot of things we really didn't intend to say. After all, you don't want the other person to get the last word. If they get the last word, it seems, you feel like you have lost the argument. And silence is a weapon and can be used in the heat of the moment. Learning how to respond and what to say when we're angry is important.

How we respond and handle things shows God and others how mature (or immature) we are. Often, God is telling us just to be quiet. We can save ourselves many troubles and sorrows by the simple act of shutting our mouths.

The Word of God tells us in the book of James:

But the tongue can no man tame; it is an unruly evil, full of deadly poison.

James 3:8

With little effort, the words we allow to pass our lips can destroy families and friendships. Hold your tongue and, instead of having to win every argument, put your energy to work accomplishing something meaningful. Get started doing what you know is needful, and you will be surprised how much you can do.

A SOFT ANSWER TURNS AWAY WRATH,
BUT HARSH WORDS STIR UP ANGER.

— Proverbs 15:1

BUT THE TONGUE CAN NO MAN TAME;
IT IS AN UNRULY EVIL,
FULL OF DEADLY POISON.

—James 3:8

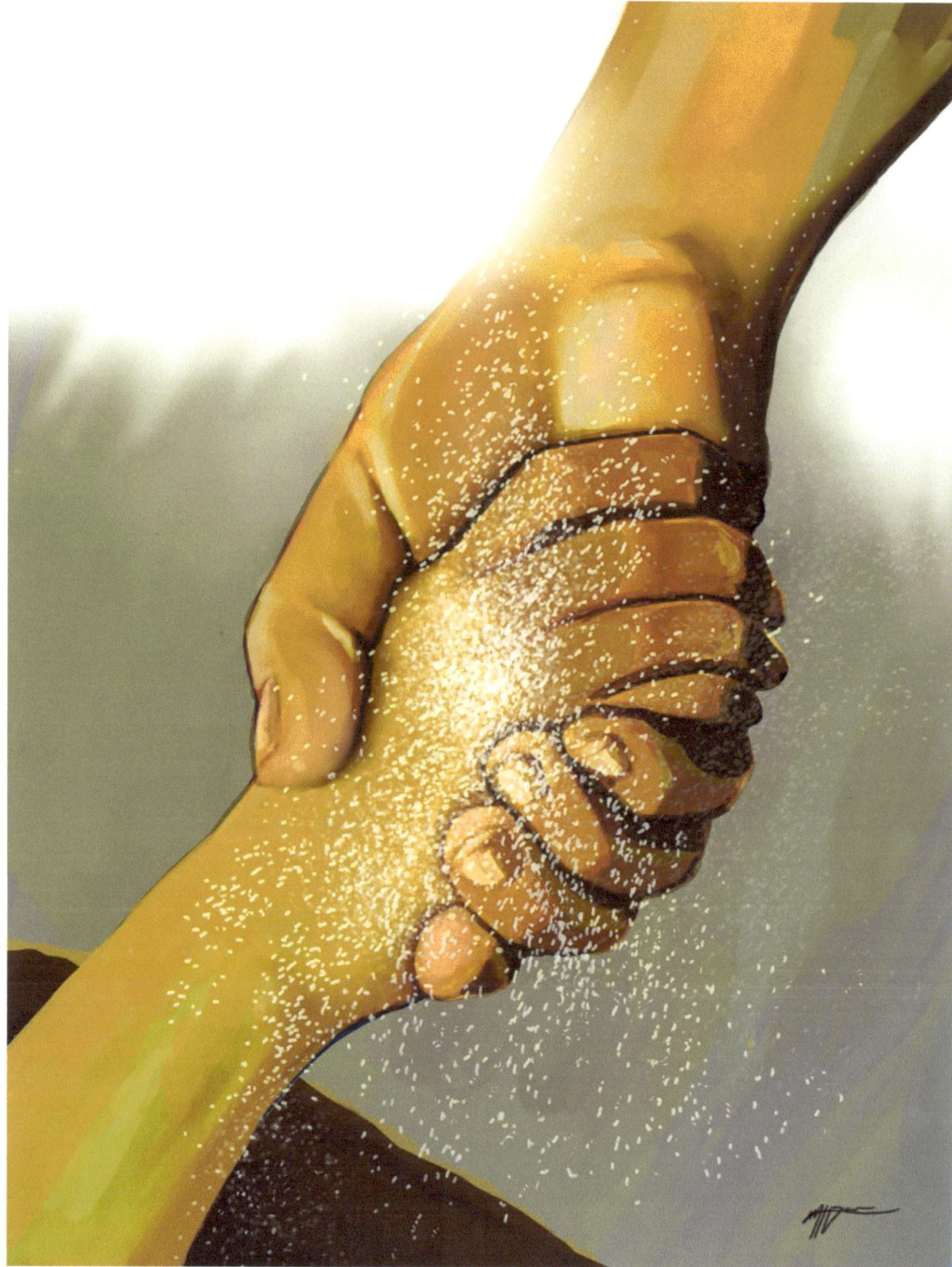

Chapter 7

Applying Yourself

Our responses are vital. We must seek the Lord and ask Him to help us with our mouths. He can help us speak life and peace into our situations and our lives.

We must believe in ourselves. Often our self-esteem is low, and that is the culprit that keeps us from making a start. We must remember that this is a trick or scheme of the enemy, so that we will remain stagnate in a place of defeat.

In my youth, I often found myself in places of defeat and didn't believe in myself enough to start something. My self-confidence was little to none.

I was on the Junior Varsity basketball team at Mount Pleasant High School, home of the Mighty Rattlers, but I struggled to find a place on the team because of my low self-esteem and lack of self-confidence. This was compounded by my overhearing some cruel words: "They're not going to play anyway, so they don't even matter," and the person saying this chuckled.

These words were spoken by one of my teammates who was, at the time, in what was considered to be the first string, the starting five. I, on the other hand, was sitting on the bench, part of the group known as the third string. Another name for us was "Bench Warmers." We were the ones who hardly ever got any PT (playing time), unless the team had a big lead and the score was up fifteen or twenty points.

Overhearing those negative words tore me to pieces. What should I do?

I made the decision not to confront these girls, and, instead, I used what they said in a positive way to help build my confidence. Marcus Garvey is quoted as saying, "If you have no confidence in self, you are twice defeated in the race of life. With confidence, you have won even before you have started."[1]

The tables were turned the next year. I sought the Lord on the matter and prayed and began to apply myself. I was told by one of my coaches in middle school in Long Beach, New York, that I had potential, if only I would apply myself. He said, "Apply yourself, young lady, and you are going to be a great basketball player one day." These words he spoke were so positive that I begin to practice. I practiced all summer and sought God on the journey to become a great basketball player. Yes. it took time, patience, and endurance, but all that challenging work paid off. I ended up moving up, not only being one of the the starting five

of Junior Varsity, but I also had the opportunity to play in varsity games.

Playing varsity games was a big jump and showed that you had some skills. I received many awards and accolades because I applied myself. I had not known about the talents and gifts that were trapped on the inside of me.

Application must also be applied concerning the Word of God in our lives. The Word of God is *"a lamp unto my feet and a light unto my path"* (Psalm 119:105). There are clearly no shortcuts or ways around application. The question is will you apply what you have heard or learned, what God is saying to you through His Word?

Applying what you have learned takes consistency. God is looking to see if we mean what we say, not with mere lip service, but with our actions. Our actions show Him our hearts. This is what He said in His Word:

These people honor me with their lips, but their hearts are far from me.　　**Matthew 15:8**

---

1. https://shoppeblack.us/marcus-garvey-quotes/#:~:text=%E2%80%9CTake%20advantage%20of%20 every%20opportunity,in%20the%20race%20of%20life.%E2%80%9D

Actions speak louder than words. You can say you are going to do this or that all day long for many days, months, and even years. It is not until it is actually done that it will be counted.

Consistency is the key when you decide in your heart to do a thing and you develop a pattern and stay with it until it becomes habitual. Some people call it faithfulness or loyalty. God is looking for that in His people.

Consistency is important to be the salt of the earth. How else do you think you will be able to win unbelievers over? The mentality should be this: as long as you given the opportunity, meaning you have God-given breath in your body, you will can keep showing up and give it your best. This gives you the opportunity to show others that you are the salt of the earth.

Keep spreading that salt by showing others the love of God in you. Let your light shine. Encourage, uplift, and inspire others by showing them what God gave you to share with the world. Many times, it requires only a soft gesture, a smile, a simple hello. A simple act of love and kindness shown to someone who is going through and needs that kindness can help them to push through and not give up.

A small act is big in someone else's world. Many times, we stand in judgment of others and don't have the authority to do so. We don't have a place to put the individual, so we should not even begin to dictate this or that.

We don't know the next person's struggles. Therefore, we should not be so quick to pass judgment upon them, as if we had already arrived and had not experienced similar struggles or even worse. Let us remember to be empathetic as it relates to our sisters and brothers.

When you want to give up, read the Word of God. Meditate on it and recite it in your mind and in your heart. Remember: you can do all things through Christ who strengthens you (see Philippians 4:13).

Chapter 8

Loving Enough

Action is love in its purest form. Showing up for people speaks so loudly. Love is the answer and has always been the answer. The greatest way to express your love is to show it. Caring and being there for someone is one of the greatest expressions of love, and it requires no words.

You have spoken so many words. Now make the effort to be there. That will be worth a billion words. Love is salt and is necessary to perform well in the Body of Christ.

In order to run well, cars must be serviced regularly. This catches any problems or underlying issues that could cause problems later. The same is true of our relationship with God. Spiritual disciplines are necessary to help us be the salt we are called to be.

Prayer, fasting, studying the Word of God and meditating on the Word are all important. The Salter is the Source that produces the salt so it can have a continual flow.

But salt must remain what it is—salt. It cannot take on the form of something else and then try to perform and be great as that something else. Salt cannot be pepper. Since its original state and purpose is to be salt, it cannot be pepper or any other seasoning and expect to perform well. Salt must be salt by keeping its original form and fulfilling its original purpose. The same is true of us as the Body of Christ. God wants us to be ORIGINAL and do things the way He intended them to be done.

The Body of Christ seems to be filled with counterfeits, and God is calling us back to walk in the calling He has purposed and ordained for us. He has made every one of His creations beautiful and unique. He created everyone different, to fulfill different purposes, and, together, spread His salt in the earth realm. In doing this, we must allow ourselves to align with His will for our lives, and then the salt (love) begins to spill over into the lives of others and becomes a blessing to them too.

God has given each of us so much salt (love) that we could never run out. His love for us is unconditional. He is the Salter and the Source of our salt. His love for us is without limitations. His Word asks and answers the question *"who can separate us"*?

"Who shall separate us from the love of Christ? Shall trouble or hardship or persecution or famine or nakedness or danger or sword? For I am convinced that neither death nor life, neither angels nor demons, neither the present nor the future, nor any powers, *neither height nor depth, nor anything else in all creation, will be able to separate us from the love of God that is in Christ Jesus our Lord.*   Romans 8:35 and 38-39

We may suffer some of those things, but the love of God is greater than anything.

God has given us the command to love Him, and He said the second command is like the first:

"And the second is like it: 'Love your neighbor as yourself.'"   Matthew 22:39

What is stopping us from salting the earth, spreading the love of God in the ways that He intended us to do? It could be in our responses. How is your reaction to certain situations in life? Do you want a different response? Then, change, and respond in a unique way.

Could it be that the way you respond to that individual or situation could be the deciding factor in their decision to follow Christ? That person may be receiving the wrong messages. Are you communicating in the right way? How do they perceive you?

Are you coming off to them as being like the Lamb of God or as being like an angry bull? Make sure you are responding in the right way at all times. God will hold us accountable for the ways in which we respond to everyone and in every situation.

Do not let your bad responses hold you back from your own breakthrough. Many times, it can be a simple miscommunication, something that got perceived in the wrong way. Self can be our biggest enemy because it works against the will of God. The Word of God tells us that we must die to the sinful flesh daily.

I face death every day—yes, just as surely as I boast about you in Christ Jesus our Lord.
1 Corinthians 15:31

We must take up our individual crosses and follow Christ:

If anyone would come after me, let him deny himself and accept his cross and follow me.
Matthew 16:24

If it takes an apology, then do it. Apologize. What do you have to lose? What are you waiting for? Do the will of God, and He will show you how you are to respond.

Trust him to fulfill all the things that He said he would be concerning your lives.

Trust in the LORD with all your heart lean not unto your own understanding acknowledge him and he shall direct your paths.
Proverbs 3:5-6

Allow the Spirit of God to guide your hearts, and watch what God will do.

Our love must be a lasting oath, an eternal vow expressed at every chance we get. As long as God has gifted us with life, we should be loving and spreading the salt, being the salt of the earth.

If the problem is unforgiveness, we should get busy getting in the face of God, repenting and asking Him to remove that bad "stuff" from our hearts. Ask Him to let you see as He sees.

Ask Him to forgive you, so you can release the individual or individuals involved. Too often we hold people hostage and carry all that extra unnecessary baggage around. Release it, let it go, and be freed. REALLY GET DELIVERED so that you can excel and move on to the next levels God has for you. NO MORE EXCUSES!

When we obey God, we begin to surrender to His will for our lives, and it becomes a beautiful thing. Deliverance is so imperative and essential to the Kingdom of God. Stop thinking that you are good to go without it because you're not. You're only fooling yourself.

Get everything out of the way of what God is trying to do in your life. He cannot bring you to an expected end if you keep getting in His way. You are your biggest distraction and downfall. Let God move in your life. He knows exactly what He is doing and is more than able to perform and bring to pass all things concerning your life. What's holding you up? You are holding yourself up. You are responsible for the stagnations and the delays.

You are asking why you seem to be stuck, but you are the hold-up. Let go and let God have His way in your life, and watch what He does for you. SURRENDER, meaning to give yourself to God in everything. The Scriptures tell us:

Submit yourselves, then, to God. Resist the devil, and he will flee from you. James 4:7

TRUST IN THE LORD

WITH ALL YOUR HEART

LEAN NOT UNTO

YOUR OWN UNDERSTANDING

ACKNOWLEDGE HIM

AND HE SHALL DIRECT

YOUR PATHS.

—Proverbs 3:5-6

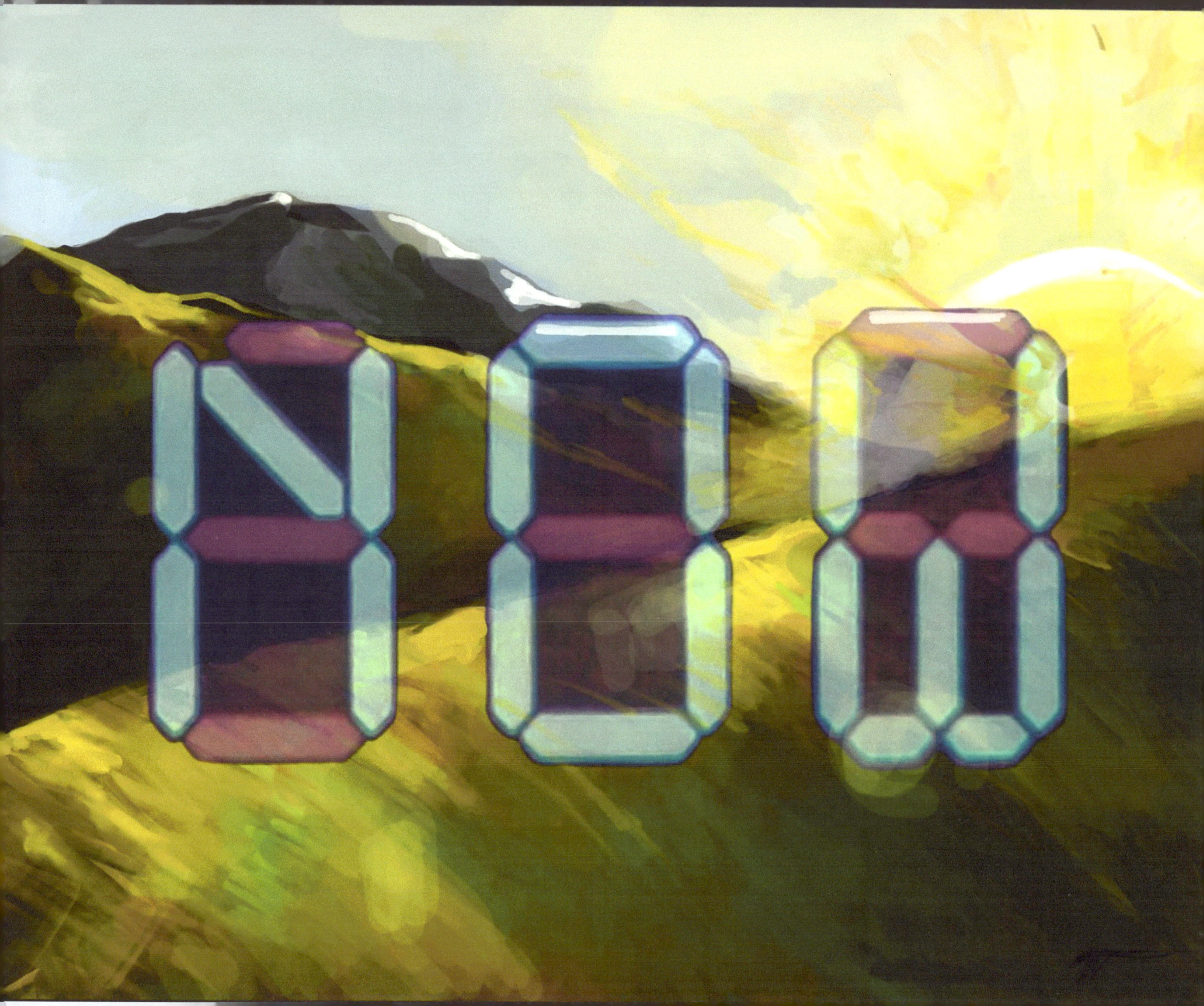

Chapter 9

Recognizing that Today Is the Day

There are no more excuses! The command that was given was for us to love God with all our hearts, minds, bodies, and souls, and the second was like the first—to love our neighbors as ourselves. Salt requires us to be active in spreading love to everyone we meet. It requires us to be the salt of the earth, as our Savior proclaimed in His Word.

Time is of the essence, so we must make the best of every opportunity that is granted to us, every chance to spread our salt. Watch the power of God transform your lives for the better. Let go of all the unnecessary things, and let God have His way.

Are you ready to love and be the salt of the earth by spreading God's love, His way, and on His terms? Do it the way God told you to, according to His leading and His instructions. You will not "mess it up" when God is orchestrating it. Show love at every opportunity, the way God intended. Be kind and gentle. Remember, give gentle answers, and don't forget to be kind. I thank God for your obedience to love under the conditions of the Holy Spirit. Remain blessed!

Now:

START APPLYING LOVE TODAY!

Author Contact Page

You may contact Michelle A. Stadard in the following way:

Mstadard@Yahoo.com

Other Books by Michelle A. Stadard

Spiritual Poems of Encouragement for the Soul

Michelle Stadard

SPIRITUAL POEMS OF ENCOURAGEMENT FOR THE SOUL

ISBN 978-1-9434091-4-3

BROKEN BUT NOT BOUND

ISBN 978-1-950398-16-4 PAPERBACK

ISBN 978-1-950398-17-1 HARDBACK

Broken but not Bound

Poems of Healing and Deliverance

WRITTEN BY MICHELLE STADARD

ILLUSTRATIONS BY TERRANCE MCDOW AND OMANI J. STADARD

www.ingramcontent.com/pod-product-compliance
Lightning Source LLC
Chambersburg PA
CBHW040452100426
42813CB00021BA/2980